COSTA BRAVA TRAVEL GUIDE 2023-2024

Your Ultimate Guide to Unveiling the Treasures of South Brava

DAISY ROBSON

Copyright © 2023 by DAISY ROBSON
All rights reserved. No part of this publication may be reproduced, distributed, or transmitted in any form or by any means, including photocopying, recording, or other electronic or mechanical methods, without the prior written permission of the publisher, except in the case of brief quotations embodied in critical reviews and certain other noncommercial uses permitted by copyright law.

Contents

INTRODUCTION 12

CHAPTER 1 18

OVERVIEW OF COSTA BRAVA 18

   History Of Costa Brava 18

   Purpose Of The Travel Guide 22

   Getting To Costa Brava 24

      Air Travel: 24

      Ground Transportation: 26

   Traveling Within Costa Brava 27

      Buses: 27

      Trains: 28

      Rental Cars: 28

      Taxis: 29

      Cycling: 29

      Walking: 30

CHAPTER 2 31

BEST TIME TO VISIT 31

   Weather And Climate 31

   Peak And Off-Peak Seasons 32

    Considerations For Costa Brava: 35
CHAPTER 3 37
SPECIAL EVENTS AND FESTIVALS 37
    Carnival 37
    Sant Joan 37
    Girona Flower Festival 38
    Costa Brava Music Festival 38
    Christmas Markets 39
CHAPTER 4 40
EXPLORING COSTA BRAVA 40
    Popular Cities And Towns 40
        Girona: 40
        Tossa de Mar: 42
        Cadaqués: 44
        Roses: 45
        Blanes: 46
        Empuriabrava 48
        Begur: 49
    Beaches And Coastal Areas 51
        Calella de Palafrugell: 51

Tossa de Mar: 51

Platja d'Aro: 52

Cadaqués: 53

L'Escala: 54

Cultural And Historical Sites 54

The Ruins of Empúries: 54

The Dali Theatre-Museum (Figueres): 55

Girona Cathedral: 55

Sant Pere de Rodes Monastery: 56

The Castle of Peralada: 56

The Jewish Quarter (Girona): 57

Sant Feliu de Guíxols Monastery: 57

Medieval Walls of Tossa de Mar: 57

Outdoor Activities And Natural Parks 58

Natural Park of Cap de Creus: 58

Montgrí, Medes Islands, and Baix Ter Natural Park 59

Aiguamolls de l'Empordà Natural Park: 59

Garrotxa Volcanic Zone Natural Park: 59

Outdoor Activities 60

    Hiking and Mountain Biking 60

    Water Sports 60

    Rock Climbing 61

    Paragliding 61

    Golf 61

CHAPTER 5 62

GASTRONOMY AND CULINARY EXPERIENCES 62

    Seafood Delicacies: 62

    Empordà Wines: 63

    Traditional Catalan Cuisine: 63

    Michelin-Starred Restaurants: 64

    Local Markets And Food Festivals: 64

    Cooking Workshops And Culinary Experiences: 65

    Farm-To-Table Experiences: 65

CHAPTER 6 67

ACCOMMODATION OPTIONS 67

    Hotels And Resorts: 67

        Hotel Santa Marta (Lloret de Mar) 67

        Hotel Vistabella (Roses) 68

Rigat Park & Spa Hotel (Lloret de Mar) 68
Vacation Rentals And Apartments: 68
    Airbnb 69
    HomeAway 69
Bed And Breakfasts: 69
    El Racó de Madremanya (Madremanya) 70
    Can Bassa (Riudarenes) 70
Camping And Caravan Parks 70
    Camping Internacional de Calonge (Calonge) 71
    Camping Riembau (Platja d'Aro) 71
Boutique Hotels: 71
    Hotel Aiguaclara (Begur) 71
    Hotel Hostalillo (Tamariu) 72
Rural Guesthouses: 72
    Mas Salvi (Pals) 72
    Can Muni (Besalú) 73
Eco-Lodges And Agrotourism: 73
    Mas Pineda (Sant Pere Pescador) 73
    Can M au (Garrigoles 74

CHAPTER 7 75
TRAVEL ITINERARIES 75
- One Week In Costa Brava 75
- Two Weeks In Costa Brava 81
  - Week 1: 81
  - Week 2: 83
- Family-Friendly Itinerary 85
- Adventure And Outdoor Activities Itinerary ... 88

CHAPTER 8 93
PRACTICAL INFORMATION 93
- Currency And Money Matters: 93
- Language And Communication: 94
- Health And Safety: 94
- Customs And Etiquette: 95

CHAPTER 9 97
TRAVEL TIPS AND RECOMMENDATIONS 97
- Must-See Attractions In Costa Brava: 97
  - Dali Theatre-Museum (Figueres) 97
  - Tossa de Mar 97
  - Girona 97

- Cap de Creus Natural Park 98
- Cadaqués: 98
- Hidden Gems In Costa Brava: 98
  - Begur 98
  - Cala S'Alguer (Palamos) 99
  - Sant Martí d'Empúries 99
  - Monastery of Sant Pere de Rodes 99
- Local Experiences And Activities 100
  - Wine Tasting in Empordà 100
  - Local Food Tours 100
  - Traditional Festivals 100
  - Outdoor Concerts and Performances 101
  - Water Sports and Sailing 101
- CHAPTER 10 102
- SHOPPING AND SOUVENIRS 102
  - Local Markets 102
  - Handcrafted Goods 102
  - Gastronomic Souvenirs 103
  - Art And Photography 103
- CHAPTER 11 104

PHOTOGRAPHY AND INSTAGRAM SPOTS 104

    Els Àngels Sanctuary (Girona) 104

    Cala Banys (Lloret De Mar) 104

    Besalú 105

    Sant Sebastià Lighthouse (Llafranc) 105

    Cap Roig Botanical Garden (Calella De Palafrugell) 105

INTRODUCTION

Once upon a time, in a cozy little town nestled among the rolling hills, there lived a young woman named Emily. Emily had always been an avid traveler, seeking new adventures and discovering the wonders of the world. One day, as she was browsing through a local bookstore, she stumbled upon a vibrant travel guide titled "Costa Brava Guide 2023-2024."

Intrigued by the colorful cover and the promise of an unforgettable journey, Emily decided to purchase the guide. Little did she know that this guide would ignite her wanderlust and take her on an extraordinary expedition.

Emily returned home and settled comfortably on her couch with a cup of tea, ready to embark on a virtual exploration of Costa Brava. As she flipped through the pages, she found herself engrossed in the vivid descriptions, captivating photographs, and detailed itineraries that awaited her.

The guide painted a picture of pristine beaches with crystal-clear waters, charming coastal towns with colorful houses, and historical sites that whispered tales of the past. It showcased the diverse range of activities available, from adventurous hikes through lush national parks to leisurely strolls along the promenades, all while savoring the region's delectable cuisine.

With each page turned, Emily's imagination soared. She envisioned herself basking in the golden sunlight on secluded beaches, tasting the mouthwatering flavors of fresh seafood, and immersing herself in the rich cultural heritage of the region.

Determined to turn her dreams into reality, Emily meticulously planned her journey, taking notes on the best times to visit, the must-see attractions, and the hidden gems recommended by the guide. She carefully curated her itinerary, ensuring she could experience the magic of Costa Brava to its fullest.

Months passed, and the day of Emily's departure finally arrived. Excitement coursed through her veins as she boarded the plane that would whisk her away to the enchanting land she had read so much about.

As she stepped onto the sun-kissed shores of Costa Brava, Emily felt an instant connection. The sights, sounds, and scents enveloped her, surpassing even her wildest imagination. She explored the picturesque towns, wandered along cobblestone streets lined with quaint shops, and marveled at the architectural wonders that stood as testaments to history.

Emily ventured off the beaten path, discovering hidden coves and secret trails that rewarded her with breathtaking panoramic views. She indulged in gastronomic delights, relishing the flavors of traditional Catalan dishes and sampling local wines that danced on her palate.

But it wasn't just the beauty of the landscapes or the flavors of the cuisine that made Costa Brava special for Emily. It was the warmth of the people she encountered, their genuine hospitality, and their passion for their homeland. They shared stories, embraced her as a fellow traveler, and made her feel like a part of their community.

As Emily's journey through Costa Brava came to an end, she reflected on the transformative experience she had. The guide had been her trusted companion, guiding her through this extraordinary adventure and unveiling the hidden treasures of the region. It had become more than just a book; it had become a source of inspiration and a cherished memory.

With a heart filled with gratitude and a spirit hungry for more adventures, Emily returned home, forever carrying Costa Brava in her soul. She knew that the guide had not only ignited her wanderlust but had also sparked a lifelong love affair with travel and the magic that lies in exploring the world.

Welcome to Costa Brava, a breathtaking coastal region nestled in the northeastern part of Catalonia, Spain. Renowned for its stunning landscapes, vibrant culture, and rich history, Costa Brava offers a diverse range of experiences for travelers seeking a memorable getaway.

Stretching along the Mediterranean Sea, Costa Brava entices visitors with its picturesque beaches, crystal-clear waters, and charming coastal towns. From the bustling city of Girona to the hidden coves and rugged cliffs, this region captivates the imagination and invites exploration.

In this comprehensive travel guide, we will delve into the highlights, hidden gems, and must-see attractions that await you in Costa Brava in the years 2023-2024. Whether you're a nature enthusiast, history buff, food lover, or adventure seeker, Costa Brava has something to offer for every type of traveler.

Discover the rich history and cultural heritage of the region by exploring ancient ruins, medieval towns, and renowned museums. Dive into the world of Salvador Dalí and explore his surrealist artwork at the Dali Theatre-Museum in Figueres. Wander through the narrow streets of Girona's historic quarter, known for its well-preserved architecture and vibrant atmosphere.

Costa Brava's natural beauty is equally captivating. Explore the rugged cliffs and hidden coves of Cap de Creus Natural Park, or relax on the pristine sandy beaches of Tossa de Mar and Cadaqués. Hike along scenic trails, venture into the Pyrenees mountains for outdoor adventures, or indulge in water sports like snorkeling, kayaking, or sailing along the captivating coastline.

Immerse yourself in the local culture and indulge in the gastronomic delights of Costa Brava. From traditional Catalan cuisine to fresh seafood delicacies, this region boasts a vibrant culinary scene. Visit local markets, sample regional wines, and savor the flavors of authentic dishes prepared with local ingredients.

As you navigate through this travel guide, you'll find comprehensive information on transportation, weather, accommodations, local customs, and a variety of itineraries to suit different interests and travel durations. Whether you're planning a family vacation, romantic getaway, or solo adventure, let this guide be your companion in discovering the wonders of Costa Brava.

CHAPTER 1
OVERVIEW OF COSTA BRAVA

History Of Costa Brava

The history of Costa Brava is a tale that weaves together the stories of ancient civilizations, conquests, cultural exchange, and the development of tourism. This beautiful coastal region of northeastern Spain, located in the province of Girona, has a rich and diverse historical background that spans thousands of years.

Prehistoric Times:

The earliest evidence of human presence in the Costa Brava region dates back to the Paleolithic period. Archaeological sites, such as the Caves of Serinyà, reveal the existence of hunter-gatherer communities who thrived in the area more than 20,000 years ago.

Roman Occupation:

During the 2nd century BCE, the Romans established their presence in the Iberian Peninsula. The Costa Brava region, then known as Hispania Tarraconensis, became part of the Roman Empire. The Romans built cities, such as Empúries, which served as an important trading hub and a gateway for the Romanization of the Iberian Peninsula.

Medieval Period:

In the early medieval period, the region witnessed the decline of the Roman Empire and the influx of different cultures. The Visigoths, a Germanic tribe, settled in the area until their kingdom fell to the Islamic conquests in the 8th century. The Muslim rule in the region lasted until the 9th century when Charlemagne's forces conquered it as part of the Carolingian Empire.

The County of Empúries:

During the 10th century, the County of Empúries emerged as an independent feudal state within the larger County of Barcelona. Empúries flourished as a maritime power, engaging in trade and establishing commercial connections throughout the Mediterranean.

The Catalan-Aragonese Union:

In the 12th century, the County of Barcelona and the Kingdom of Aragon united through the marriage of Ramon Berenguer IV and Petronilla of Aragon. This union laid the foundation for the formation of the Crown of Aragon, which expanded its influence and controlled territories including Costa Brava.

Pirates and Maritime Conflicts:

Throughout the Middle Ages, Costa Brava experienced periods of insecurity due to pirate attacks and conflicts between different Mediterranean powers. The region's coastal towns, such as Tossa de Mar, fortified themselves to protect against pirate raids.

Modern Era and Artistic Influence:

In the 19th and 20th centuries, Costa Brava experienced significant transformations. Industrialization and the expansion of railway networks contributed to the growth of tourism, attracting visitors from around the world. The picturesque landscapes and the region's artistic charm attracted prominent artists, including Salvador Dalí, who was born in Figueres, a town in Costa Brava. Dalí's influence and the establishment of the Dalí Theatre-Museum in Figueres brought international attention to the region's artistic and cultural heritage.

Tourism Boom:

Since the mid-20th century, Costa Brava has become one of the most popular tourist destinations in Spain. The stunning coastline, with its pristine beaches and charming seaside towns, draws millions of visitors each year. Coastal cities like Lloret de Mar and Tossa de Mar have developed into vibrant resorts, offering a wide range of accommodations, recreational activities, and entertainment options

Purpose Of The Travel Guide

Destination Familiarization: The travel guide introduces readers to Costa Brava, providing an overview of the region's geography, history, culture, and attractions. It helps travelers gain a deeper understanding of the destination, enabling them to appreciate its unique characteristics and make informed decisions about their itinerary.

Trip Planning Assistance: Planning a trip can be overwhelming, especially when exploring a new destination. The travel guide acts as a roadmap, assisting travelers in organizing their journey. It offers guidance on the best times to visit, popular attractions to include in the itinerary, and lesser-known hidden gems worth exploring. By presenting different travel itineraries and suggestions, the guide helps travelers optimize their time and make the most of their visit to Costa Brava.

Practical Information and Logistics: Travel guides provide essential practical information to ensure a smooth and hassle-free trip. They offer details on transportation options, including air travel, ground transportation, and local public transport systems. Additionally, they provide insights into accommodation options, ranging from hotels and resorts to vacation rentals and camping sites. The guide also addresses important logistics such as currency, language, communication, health and safety tips, customs, and etiquette, enabling travelers to be well-prepared for their journey.

Cultural and Historical Insights: Costa Brava is a region rich in cultural and historical heritage. A travel guide delves into the traditions, festivals, and local customs, giving travelers a deeper appreciation of the local culture. It highlights historical sites, museums, and architectural landmarks, shedding light on the region's past and offering a glimpse into its evolution. By understanding the cultural context, travelers can engage with the local community, immerse themselves in the destination, and create meaningful connections.

Recommendations and Insider Tips: A travel guide provides recommendations on must-see attractions, dining options, shopping opportunities, and off-the-beaten-path experiences. It highlights local specialties, traditional dishes, and gastronomic delights, allowing travelers to savor the authentic flavors of the region. Insider tips, based on local knowledge and firsthand experiences, help visitors navigate through the destination with valuable insights, ensuring they don't miss out on hidden gems or fall into common tourist traps.

Inspiration and Wanderlust: Travel guides evoke a sense of wanderlust and inspire readers to embark on their own adventures. Through captivating descriptions, vibrant photographs, and engaging storytelling, they ignite the imagination, fueling the desire to explore new places. The travel guide for Costa Brava serves as a source of inspiration, encouraging travelers to discover the region's natural beauty, cultural treasures, and unforgettable experiences.

Getting To Costa Brava

Air Travel:
The most common way to access Costa Brava from international or domestic locations is by air.

The region is served by several airports, each offering varying degrees of connectivity.

a. Barcelona El Prat Airport (BCN): Situated approximately 80 kilometers south of Costa Brava, Barcelona El Prat Airport is the primary international gateway to the region. It offers a wide range of flights from major airlines worldwide. From the airport, travelers can easily reach Costa Brava by various means, including car rentals, private transfers, or public transportation.

b. Girona-Costa Brava Airport (GRO): Located near the city of Girona, this airport serves as a convenient entry point for Costa Brava. It is well-connected to various European destinations and caters to budget airlines. From Girona-Costa Brava Airport, travelers can access different parts of Costa Brava using ground transportation options such as buses, taxis, or rental cars.

c. Perpignan-Rivesaltes Airport (PGF): Situated just across the French border, Perpignan-Rivesaltes Airport provides another option for accessing Costa Brava. It serves as an entry point for travelers coming from France or other European countries. From the airport, travelers can connect to Costa Brava via ground transportation options, including buses or rental cars.

Ground Transportation:

Once travelers arrive at the nearest airport, various ground transportation options are available to reach different destinations within Costa Brava.

a. Trains: The Spanish railway network, operated by Renfe, provides train services connecting major cities and towns in Costa Brava. The high-speed train (AVE) network links Barcelona and Girona to other Spanish cities, making it a convenient option for those arriving at Barcelona El Prat Airport. Regional and local trains also operate within the region, providing access to smaller towns and coastal areas.

b. Buses: Bus services are a popular mode of transportation for traveling within Costa Brava. Companies such as Sarfa and Moventis operate regular bus routes that connect major cities, towns, and coastal areas in the region. Buses offer an affordable and flexible option for getting around, allowing travelers to explore different parts of Costa Brava at their own pace.

c. Taxis and Private Transfers: Taxis and private transfers provide a convenient and comfortable option for reaching specific destinations within Costa Brava. Taxis can be found at airports and major transportation hubs, while private transfer services can be pre-booked for a personalized and hassle-free experience.

d. Rental Cars: Renting a car is a popular choice for travelers who prefer flexibility and independence. Several car rental companies operate at airports and major cities, offering a wide range of vehicles to suit different needs. Having a rental car allows travelers to explore the region at their own pace and visit off-the-beaten-path locations.

Traveling Within Costa Brava

Buses:

Costa Brava has a well-developed bus network that connects its towns, villages, and coastal areas. Buses are a popular and affordable option for traveling within the region. Companies such as Sarfa and Moventis operate regular bus routes, offering convenient connections between major cities like Girona and coastal towns like Lloret de Mar, Tossa de Mar, and Cadaqués. Buses provide scenic routes, allowing travelers to soak in the coastal beauty and explore different parts of Costa Brava.

Trains:

The Spanish railway network, operated by Renfe, provides train services that connect major cities in Costa Brava. The high-speed train (AVE) network offers connections between Barcelona and Girona, making it a convenient option for traveling to and from the region. Regional and local trains also operate within Costa Brava, serving towns like Blanes, Figueres, and Palamós. Trains offer comfort and efficiency, allowing travelers to reach their destinations while enjoying the scenic landscapes.

Rental Cars:

Renting a car provides flexibility and independence, allowing travelers to explore Costa Brava at their own pace. Major car rental companies have offices at airports and cities within the region. Having a rental car gives you the freedom to discover hidden gems, visit off-the-beaten-path locations, and enjoy the scenic coastal drives. It is important to familiarize yourself with local traffic rules and parking regulations before embarking on your road trip.

Taxis:

Taxis are widely available in Costa Brava and can be found at airports, major transportation hubs, and in city centers. Taxis provide convenience and comfort, especially for short distances or when traveling with luggage. It is advisable to use licensed taxis and confirm the fare or request to use the meter before starting the journey. Taxis are also a good option for day trips or transportation between towns when you prefer not to drive.

Cycling:

Costa Brava offers a picturesque landscape that is perfect for cycling enthusiasts. Many towns provide bicycle rental services, allowing travelers to explore the region on two wheels. Cycling routes, both on-road and off-road, cater to different levels of experience and lead to beautiful coastal paths, charming villages, and scenic countryside areas. Cycling allows for a more immersive experience, allowing you to connect with nature and enjoy the region's beauty at a leisurely pace.

Walking:

For those who enjoy a slower pace and want to immerse themselves in the charm of Costa Brava, walking is an excellent option. Many towns have compact city centers that can easily be explored on foot, allowing you to discover narrow streets, historic buildings, and local markets. Walking along the coastal paths provides breathtaking views of the Mediterranean Sea, hidden coves, and rugged cliffs. Hiking trails in natural parks like Cap de Creus and Montgrí offer opportunities to explore the region's diverse landscapes.

CHAPTER 2
BEST TIME TO VISIT

Weather And Climate

Spring (March to May): Spring in Costa Brava brings mild temperatures and blossoming landscapes. Average temperatures range from 10°C to 20°C (50°F to 68°F), making it an ideal time for outdoor activities such as hiking and exploring the region's natural beauty. Spring also offers fewer crowds compared to the peak summer season.

Summer (June to August): Summers in Costa Brava are warm to hot, with average temperatures ranging from 20°C to 30°C (68°F to 86°F). This is the peak tourist season when the region sees an influx of visitors looking to enjoy the beaches, water activities, and vibrant coastal towns. It is advisable to pack sunscreen, hats, and light clothing to stay comfortable during the summer months.

Autumn (September to November): Autumn brings mild temperatures, making it another pleasant season to visit Costa Brava. Average temperatures range from 15°C to 25°C (59°F to 77°F). The region experiences fewer crowds during this time, allowing travelers to explore popular attractions without the hustle and bustle of the summer season. Autumn is also a great time for wine enthusiasts, as the vineyards in the region are in full harvest mode.

Winter (December to February): Winter in Costa Brava is characterized by cool temperatures, with average highs ranging from 10°C to 15°C (50°F to 59°F). While it may be too cold for beach activities, the region offers a unique charm during this season. Travelers can explore historic sites, indulge in local cuisine, and enjoy cultural events and festivals that take place during the winter months.

Peak And Off-Peak Seasons

Peak and off-peak seasons refer to periods of high and low demand for tourism in a particular destination. Understanding these seasons can help travelers plan their trips more effectively, taking into account factors such as crowd levels, availability of accommodations, and pricing.

Peak Season:

Peak season is characterized by the highest demand for travel to a destination. It typically corresponds to periods when schools are on vacation, and weather conditions are favorable. During peak season, popular tourist destinations can be crowded, accommodations may be limited, and prices for flights and accommodations tend to be higher. Some key factors associated with peak season include:

High Demand: Peak season attracts a large number of tourists seeking to explore a destination's attractions and enjoy its favorable weather conditions. This can result in crowded tourist sites, longer queues, and a bustling atmosphere.

Favorable Weather: Peak season often aligns with a destination's best weather, such as warm summers or mild winters. This is particularly relevant for coastal regions like Costa Brava, where visitors are drawn to the beaches and outdoor activities.

School Vacations: Families with school-age children tend to travel during school breaks, contributing to the increased demand during peak season. This can lead to higher prices and limited availability of family-oriented accommodations and attractions.

Off-Peak Season:

Off-peak season refers to periods when there is lower demand for travel to a destination. It is characterized by fewer tourists, more affordable prices, and a quieter atmosphere.

Lower Crowds: Off-peak season offers the advantage of fewer tourists, allowing travelers to explore popular attractions with more ease and without the hustle and bustle of peak season. This can enhance the overall travel experience and provide a more relaxed atmosphere.

Cost Savings: Prices for flights, accommodations, and activities tend to be lower during off-peak season due to reduced demand. Travelers can take advantage of discounted rates and special offers, allowing them to stretch their budget further.

Unique Experiences: Off-peak season often provides opportunities to engage more intimately with the local culture and community. Travelers may have more interaction with locals, find greater availability for tours and activities, and experience special events or festivals that are unique to the off-peak period.

Considerations For Costa Brava:

Costa Brava, with its beautiful coastline, charming towns, and mild climate, experiences distinct peak and off-peak seasons:

Peak Season: In Costa Brava, the peak season generally occurs during the summer months of June, July, and August. This period coincides with school vacations and offers warm weather, making it an ideal time for beach activities, water sports, and exploring coastal towns. Popular destinations like Lloret de Mar, Tossa de Mar, and

Cadaqués can be crowded, and it is advisable to book accommodations and activities well in advance.

Off-Peak Season: The off-peak seasons in Costa Brava include spring (March to May) and autumn (September to November). During these periods, the weather remains pleasant, though not as hot as in summer. Travelers can enjoy quieter beaches, explore inland towns, and indulge in local cuisine. The off-peak seasons offer more affordable prices for accommodations, and attractions are less crowded, allowing for a more relaxed and immersive experience.

CHAPTER 3
SPECIAL EVENTS AND FESTIVALS

Costa Brava hosts a variety of special events and festivals throughout the year, adding to the vibrant and festive atmosphere of the region. Some notable events include:

Carnival

Held in February or early March, Carnival celebrations take place in various towns and cities throughout Costa Brava. Colorful parades, costumes, music, and dancing are a highlight of these festivities.

Sant Joan

Celebrated on the night of June 23rd, Sant Joan marks the beginning of summer with bonfires, fireworks, music, and dancing on the beaches.

This traditional celebration is known for its lively atmosphere and is a favorite among locals and visitors alike.

Girona Flower Festival

Taking place in May, the Girona Flower Festival transforms the city of Girona into a colorful and fragrant spectacle. The streets, squares, and buildings are adorned with stunning floral displays, creating a magical ambiance.

Costa Brava Music Festival

Held during the summer months, the Costa Brava Music Festival attracts renowned national and international musicians who perform in various venues across the region. Classical, jazz, and contemporary music enthusiasts will find a range of performances to enjoy.

Christmas Markets

During the holiday season, many towns and cities in Costa Brava host charming Christmas markets where visitors can explore stalls selling crafts, local products, and delicious treats. The markets often feature festive decorations, live music, and a joyful atmosphere.

CHAPTER 4
EXPLORING COSTA BRAVA

Popular Cities And Towns

Girona:

Girona is a captivating city that showcases a rich history and cultural heritage. Its well-preserved medieval architecture, cobblestone streets, and ancient walls make it a popular destination in Costa Brava. Some notable attractions in Girona include:

Girona Cathedral: The imposing Girona Cathedral, also known as the Cathedral of Santa Maria, is a magnificent example of Gothic architecture. Its grandeur and intricate details, including the widest Gothic nave in the world, leave visitors in awe.

The Jewish Quarter (El Call): Explore the narrow streets of the Jewish Quarter, one of the best-preserved in Europe. This area holds historical significance and offers a glimpse into the city's Jewish heritage.

Arab Baths (Banys Àrabs): Dating back to the 12th century, the Arab Baths are a unique relic of Girona's Moorish past. Visitors can wander through the various rooms, including the cold room, warm room, and hot room, gaining insight into ancient bathing rituals.

Onyar River: The colorful houses along the Onyar River are an iconic symbol of Girona. Strolling across the numerous bridges and admiring the vibrant facades is a delightful experience.

Lloret de Mar:

Lloret de Mar is a bustling coastal resort town known for its lively atmosphere and beautiful beaches. It offers a wide array of entertainment options and attractions, including:

Lloret Beach: The main beach in Lloret de Mar, Playa de Lloret, is a stunning stretch of golden sand fringed by crystal-clear waters. It is a hub of activity, offering water sports, beach bars, and sun loungers for relaxation.

Santa Clotilde Gardens: These beautiful gardens sit atop a cliff overlooking the sea. With manicured hedges, serene paths, and stunning views, they provide a tranquil escape from the bustling town below.

Maritime Museum: Located in an old lighthouse, the Maritime Museum offers insights into the region's seafaring history. Visitors can learn about traditional fishing techniques, explore exhibitions, and see a collection of nautical artifacts.

Castle of Sant Joan: Perched on a hill overlooking Lloret de Mar, the Castle of Sant Joan offers panoramic views of the town and the coastline. The castle's ruins and scenic surroundings make it a popular spot for sightseeing.

Tossa de Mar:

Tossa de Mar is a charming coastal town known for its medieval fortress and picturesque beaches. Here are some highlights of this idyllic destination:

Vila Vella (Old Town): Enclosed by ancient walls, Vila Vella is a well-preserved medieval fortress. Its narrow streets, whitewashed houses, and stunning views of the Mediterranean create a magical atmosphere. Explore the charming shops, dine at traditional restaurants, and visit the lighthouse for breathtaking panoramas.

Tossa Beaches: Tossa de Mar boasts several beautiful beaches. Playa Gran is the main beach, offering golden sands and calm waters. For a quieter atmosphere, head to Playa d'es Codolar or hike along the coastal paths to discover hidden coves.

Municipal Museum: Located within the fortified walls of Vila Vella, the Municipal Museum provides insights into the town's history and art. It houses a collection of contemporary and traditional artworks, archaeological exhibits, and displays on local traditions.

Camí de Ronda: The Camí de Ronda is a scenic coastal path that connects Tossa de Mar with neighboring beaches and coves. Walking along the path offers stunning views of the rugged coastline, and it's an excellent way to explore the natural beauty of the region.

Cadaqués:

Cadaqués is a picturesque fishing village that has long been a haven for artists and intellectuals. Its charm lies in its whitewashed houses, narrow streets, and stunning waterfront. Here are some highlights of Cadaqués:

Salvador Dalí House-Museum: Cadaqués is closely associated with the renowned artist Salvador Dalí, who spent much of his life in the village. The Salvador Dalí House-Museum, located in Portlligat, is where he lived and worked. Visitors can explore the quirky rooms and learn about Dalí's life and artistic process.

Church of Santa Maria: The Church of Santa Maria, located in the heart of Cadaqués, is a beautiful example of Baroque architecture. Its white facade and bell tower are iconic features of the town's skyline.

Portlligat Bay: This scenic bay is a tranquil spot with crystal-clear waters. It offers opportunities for swimming, sunbathing, and enjoying the peaceful ambiance. Visitors can relax on the small pebble beach or explore the picturesque harbor.

Cap de Creus Natural Park: Cadaqués is the gateway to the stunning Cap de Creus Natural Park. This rugged peninsula is known for its unique rock formations, hidden coves, and hiking trails. Exploring the park rewards visitors with breathtaking views of the Mediterranean coastline.

Roses:

Roses is a vibrant coastal town situated on the northern end of Costa Brava. It offers a perfect blend of sandy beaches, historical sites, and natural beauty. Here are some highlights of Roses:

Citadel of Roses: The Citadel of Roses is an ancient fortress that dates back to the 4th century BC. It served as a defense against pirates and invaders and offers panoramic views of the town and the sea. Visitors can explore the archaeological site, including the remains of Roman villas and an ancient Greek colony.

Roses Beaches: Roses is renowned for its beautiful sandy beaches. Playa de la Punta is the main beach, offering a wide stretch of golden sand and various water sports activities. Other notable beaches include Canyelles Petites, Almadrava, and

Santa Margarida, each with its own unique charm and amenities.

Santa Maria de Roses: The parish church of Santa Maria de Roses is a notable religious site in the town. It features a blend of architectural styles, including Gothic, Renaissance, and Baroque. Inside, visitors can admire the beautiful altarpiece and other religious artifacts.

Cap de Creus: Roses is the gateway to the stunning Cap de Creus Natural Park, which is known for its rugged cliffs, hidden coves, and pristine landscapes. The lighthouse at Cap de Creus offers breathtaking views of the surrounding coastline and the Mediterranean Sea. Exploring the park's hiking trails allows visitors to discover the unique flora and fauna of the area.

Blanes:

Blanes is a coastal town located at the southernmost point of Costa Brava. It is known for its vibrant atmosphere, beautiful gardens, and annual fireworks festival. Here are some highlights of Blanes:

Marimurtra Botanical Garden: Marimurtra Botanical Garden is one of the most stunning gardens in the Mediterranean. It showcases a wide variety of plant species from around the world and offers breathtaking views of the sea. The garden's terraces, water features, and meticulously maintained plants make it a peaceful oasis.

Blanes Beaches: Blanes boasts several beautiful beaches where visitors can relax and enjoy the sun. The main beach, Playa de Blanes, offers a long stretch of golden sand and a range of water sports activities. Other notable beaches include Cala Bona, Cala Sant Francesc, and Treumal, each with its own distinct character.

Castle of Sant Joan: Perched on a hill overlooking Blanes, the Castle of Sant Joan is a medieval fortress that offers panoramic views of the town and the coastline. Visitors can explore the castle's ruins and learn about its historical significance.

International Fireworks Competition: Blanes hosts an annual international fireworks competition, known as the Concurso Internacional de Fuegos Artificiales. This spectacular event attracts pyrotechnic teams from around the world who compete to create the most impressive fireworks displays. The festival takes place over several days and is a highlight for visitors during the summer months.

Empuriabrava

Empuriabrava, often referred to as the "Venice of Spain," is a unique town renowned for its intricate network of canals and marinas. It offers a distinctive coastal lifestyle and a range of water-based activities. Here are some highlights of Empuriabrava:

Canals and Marinas: The main attraction of Empuriabrava is its extensive network of canals, which are navigable by boats. The town is famous for having the largest residential marina in Europe, with thousands of private moorings. Visitors can take boat tours, rent a boat or kayak, or simply stroll along the canals to admire the waterfront properties and yachts.

Empuriabrava Beach: The town boasts a long sandy beach that stretches for several kilometers along the Mediterranean Sea. The beach offers ample space for sunbathing, beach sports, and swimming. Visitors can also enjoy beachfront restaurants and bars, providing a lively atmosphere.

Skydiving: Empuriabrava is a popular destination for skydiving enthusiasts. The town is home to Skydive Empuriabrava, one of the largest skydiving centers in Europe. Adventure seekers can experience the thrill of tandem skydiving or participate in training courses for solo jumps.

Aiguamolls de l'Empordà Natural Park: Situated near Empuriabrava, Aiguamolls de l'Empordà is a natural park of wetlands, marshes, and lagoons. It is a haven for birdwatchers, as it serves as a migratory stopover for various bird species. Visitors can explore the park's walking trails and observation points to observe the diverse birdlife and enjoy the tranquil natural surroundings.

Begur:

Begur is a charming hilltop town that offers a unique blend of history, nature, and stunning views of the coastline. Nestled in the heart of the Empordà region, Begur is known for its medieval architecture, beautiful beaches, and proximity to natural parks. Here are some highlights of Begur:

Begur Castle: The town is dominated by its medieval castle, which sits atop a hill overlooking the village and the sea. Visitors can explore the castle ruins and enjoy panoramic views of the surrounding landscapes.

Sa Riera Beach: Sa Riera is one of the most picturesque beaches in the area, located just a short distance from Begur. It boasts crystal-clear waters, golden sand, and a charming fishing village atmosphere. The beach offers various water activities and beachfront restaurants.

Aiguablava Beach: Another stunning beach near Begur is Aiguablava. It features turquoise waters, pristine white sand, and dramatic cliffs. The beach is surrounded by luxury villas and offers a tranquil setting for relaxation and sunbathing.

Natural Parks: Begur is surrounded by natural parks, including the Montgrí, Medes Islands, and Baix Ter Natural Park. These protected areas are ideal for hiking, birdwatching, and enjoying the diverse flora and fauna of the region.

Beaches And Coastal Areas

Calella de Palafrugell:

Calella de Palafrugell is a charming coastal town known for its picturesque beaches and traditional fishing village atmosphere. It offers several beautiful beaches, including:

Canadell Beach: This sandy beach is one of the most popular in Calella de Palafrugell. It is characterized by its calm waters and scenic surroundings. Visitors can relax on the beach, swim in the azure waters, or enjoy a leisurely stroll along the promenade.

Port Bo Beach: Located in the heart of the town, Port Bo Beach is a small cove with crystal-clear waters and a lively atmosphere. It is dotted with colorful fishing boats and lined with restaurants serving fresh seafood.

Tossa de Mar:

Tossa de Mar boasts some of the most picturesque beaches on the Costa Brava coastline. Here are two notable ones:

Tossa Beach: This expansive golden sandy beach is located just below the medieval walls of Tossa de Mar's old town. With its shallow waters and gentle waves, it is ideal for families and sunbathers. The beach is lined with restaurants, cafes, and shops, offering all the amenities needed for a day by the sea.

Cala Pola Beach: Nestled in a small cove, Cala Pola Beach offers a secluded and peaceful atmosphere. Surrounded by cliffs and lush greenery, it provides a stunning natural setting for sunbathing and swimming.

Platja d'Aro:

Platja d'Aro is a bustling seaside resort town known for its lively atmosphere and vibrant beach scene. It offers several sandy beaches along its extensive coastline, including:

Platja Gran: The main beach of Platja d'Aro, Platja Gran, is a wide sandy stretch that stretches for over two kilometers. It is a popular spot for sunbathing, beach sports, and water activities such as paddleboarding and kayaking. The beach is lined with beach bars, cafes, and shops, creating a lively and vibrant atmosphere.

Cala Rovira: This charming little cove is located just a short walk from Platja Gran. Surrounded by cliffs and pine trees, Cala Rovira offers a more secluded and tranquil beach experience. Its clear turquoise waters are perfect for swimming and snorkeling.

Cadaqués:

Cadaqués, a picturesque fishing village, is renowned for its unique coastal beauty. It offers several stunning beaches and coves, including:

Playa Gran: Cadaqués' main beach, Playa Gran, is a wide sandy beach with shallow, calm waters. It offers beautiful views of the surrounding landscape and is perfect for sunbathing and swimming.

Ses Oliveres Beach: This small pebble beach is tucked away in a rocky cove, offering a more secluded and intimate atmosphere. It is surrounded by olive trees and provides a peaceful setting for relaxation.

L'Escala:

L'Escala is a coastal town known for its rich history and beautiful beaches. Some notable beaches in the area include:

Riells Beach: Riells Beach is a wide sandy beach with shallow waters, making it suitable for families with children. It offers a range of water sports activities, beachfront restaurants, and shops.

Cala Montgó: This picturesque cove is located within the Montgrí Natural Park. Surrounded by cliffs and lush greenery, Cala Montgó boasts crystal-clear waters and is a popular spot for snorkeling and diving.

Cultural And Historical Sites

The Ruins of Empúries:

Located near the town of L'Escala, the Ruins of Empúries are an exceptional archaeological site that showcases the remains of an ancient Greek and Roman city. The site offers a glimpse into the region's early history and the influence of these ancient civilizations. Visitors can explore the well-preserved Greek and Roman ruins, including temples, mosaics, and an amphitheater, while learning about the significance of the site through informative exhibits.

The Dali Theatre-Museum (Figueres):

Figueres is the birthplace of one of the most renowned artists of the 20th century, Salvador Dalí. The Dali Theatre-Museum is a surrealistic masterpiece created by Dalí himself, housing an extensive collection of his works. The museum showcases Dalí's unique artistic vision and offers a surreal experience with its mind-bending exhibits, including melting clocks and bizarre sculptures. It is a must-visit for art enthusiasts and those interested in Dalí's eccentric world.

Girona Cathedral:

Girona Cathedral, also known as the Cathedral of Santa Maria, is an iconic landmark of the city. It is a stunning example of Gothic architecture and boasts an impressive set of stairs leading up to its grand entrance. Inside, visitors can marvel at the ornate chapels, a beautiful nave, and the Tapestry of Creation, a masterpiece of Romanesque embroidery. Climbing the cathedral's bell tower provides panoramic views of Girona and the surrounding landscapes.

Sant Pere de Rodes Monastery:

Perched on a hilltop overlooking the Bay of Roses, Sant Pere de Rodes is a magnificent medieval monastery. The monastery dates back to the 10th century and features a mix of architectural styles, including Romanesque and Gothic elements. Visitors can explore the various sections of the complex, including the church, cloister, and bell tower, while enjoying panoramic views of the coastline and the surrounding natural landscapes.

The Castle of Peralada:

Situated in the town of Peralada, the Castle of Peralada is a historic fortress that dates back to the 14th century. The castle boasts a rich history and is now home to a cultural complex that includes a library, wine museum, and a casino. Visitors can take guided tours of the castle, stroll through its beautiful gardens, and even catch a performance at the outdoor amphitheater during the Peralada Castle Festival.

The Jewish Quarter (Girona):

Girona's Jewish Quarter, known as the Call, is one of the best-preserved medieval Jewish quarters in Europe. Its narrow streets, charming squares, and ancient buildings take visitors back in time to the Middle Ages. The area is home to the Jewish History Museum, which provides insight into the vibrant Jewish community that once thrived in Girona. Exploring the labyrinthine streets of the Call offers a glimpse into the city's rich Jewish heritage.

Sant Feliu de Guíxols Monastery:

The Sant Feliu de Guíxols Monastery, located in the town of Sant Feliu de Guíxols, is a beautiful Benedictine monastery with a history dating back over a thousand years. The monastery complex includes a church, a cloister, and a museum. The museum houses a collection of religious art, including medieval sculptures and paintings. Visitors can also stroll through the tranquil gardens surrounding the monastery.

Medieval Walls of Tossa de Mar:

Tossa de Mar is home to a well-preserved medieval old town, enclosed by ancient walls. The fortified walls offer a glimpse into the town's history as a defensive stronghold. Within the walls, visitors can wander through narrow cobblestone streets, explore historic buildings, and admire the panoramic views of the Mediterranean Sea. The town's Vila Vella (Old Town) is also home to the Municipal Museum, which displays artifacts from Tossa de Mar's past.

Outdoor Activities And Natural Parks

Natural Park of Cap de Creus:
Located in the northeastern corner of Catalonia, the Natural Park of Cap de Creus is a rugged and wild coastal park known for its breathtaking scenery. Here, visitors can embark on hikes along the coastal paths, exploring dramatic cliffs, hidden coves, and panoramic viewpoints. The park is also home to unique flora and fauna, making it a paradise for nature lovers and birdwatchers.

Montgrí, Medes Islands, and Baix Ter Natural Park

Situated in the Empordà region, this natural park encompasses diverse ecosystems, including the Montgrí mountain range, the Medes Islands, and the Baix Ter wetlands. Outdoor enthusiasts can enjoy a range of activities, such as hiking, mountain biking, and birdwatching. The Medes Islands, a protected marine reserve, offer incredible opportunities for diving and snorkeling, with their crystal-clear waters and rich marine life.

Aiguamolls de l'Empordà Natural Park:

Aiguamolls de l'Empordà is a wetland nature reserve of international importance. The park is a haven for birdwatchers, as it serves as a vital stopover for various migratory bird species. Visitors can explore the park's walking trails, observation points, and bird hides to observe a wide array of birdlife. Additionally, the park offers guided boat tours, allowing visitors to immerse themselves in the tranquil beauty of the wetlands.

Garrotxa Volcanic Zone Natural Park:

Situated inland from the Costa Brava region, the Garrotxa Volcanic Zone Natural Park is a unique landscape characterized by extinct volcanoes, lava flows, and lush vegetation. The park offers a network of hiking trails that wind through the volcanic terrain, leading to panoramic viewpoints and hidden waterfalls. Visitors can also explore the famous Fageda d'en Jordà, a beech forest that covers the lava fields and provides a mystical atmosphere.

Outdoor Activities

Costa Brava provides ample opportunities for various outdoor activities. Some popular activities include:

Hiking and Mountain Biking
The region offers an extensive network of hiking and mountain biking trails that cater to all levels of fitness and experience. From coastal paths to mountainous terrain, there are options for every adventurer to explore the natural beauty of Costa Brava.

Water Sports
With its pristine coastline and clear waters, Costa Brava is perfect for water sports enthusiasts.

Visitors can engage in activities such as kayaking, paddleboarding, windsurfing, and sailing. There are rental facilities and schools available for beginners to learn and enjoy these exhilarating activities.

Rock Climbing

Costa Brava is a paradise for rock climbers, with its rugged cliffs and stunning sea views. There are several climbing areas throughout the region that cater to climbers of all levels, offering challenges and breathtaking vistas.

Paragliding

The hilly landscapes and coastal cliffs provide an ideal setting for paragliding. Adventurers can take off from designated launch sites and enjoy soaring through the skies while taking in panoramic views of the Costa Brava coastline.

Golf

Costa Brava is home to several world-class golf courses that offer stunning views and challenging fairways. Golf enthusiasts can enjoy a round of golf surrounded by beautiful scenery and a pleasant Mediterranean climate.

CHAPTER 5
GASTRONOMY AND CULINARY EXPERIENCES

Seafood Delicacies:

With its long coastline and vibrant fishing communities, Costa Brava is renowned for its seafood. From prawns, anchovies, and sardines to sea bass, hake, and monkfish, the region's restaurants and coastal towns offer an abundance of delectable seafood options. Don't miss the opportunity to savor traditional dishes like suquet de peix (fish stew), esqueixada (salted cod salad), and fideuà (a seafood variation of paella made with noodles).

Empordà Wines:

Costa Brava is part of the Empordà wine region, which produces a variety of exceptional wines. The region's diverse terroir, influenced by the Mediterranean climate and Tramuntana winds, creates the perfect conditions for winemaking. Wine enthusiasts can embark on wine tours and tastings at local wineries, exploring the unique flavors of Empordà wines, including reds made from Grenache and Carignan grapes, as well as whites made from varieties like Garnacha Blanca and Macabeo.

Traditional Catalan Cuisine:

Costa Brava is located in Catalonia, and therefore, visitors have the opportunity to indulge in traditional Catalan cuisine. Catalans take great pride in their culinary traditions, and Costa Brava is no exception. From hearty meat dishes like botifarra amb mongetes (sausage with white beans) and fricandó (beef stew) to iconic Catalan specialties like pa amb tomàquet (bread with tomato) and crema catalana (Catalan cream), you can savor the authentic flavors of the region.

Michelin-Starred Restaurants:

Costa Brava is home to several Michelin-starred restaurants, offering exceptional dining experiences for food enthusiasts. These establishments showcase innovative culinary techniques, local ingredients, and artistic presentations. Indulge in a gastronomic journey at renowned restaurants like El Celler de Can Roca in Girona, which has been awarded three Michelin stars, or discover hidden gems that have earned their well-deserved Michelin recognition.

Local Markets And Food Festivals:

The region's markets offer a wide range of fresh produce, local cheeses, cured meats, and other delicacies. Explore the Mercat Municipal in Girona or the Mercat de la Boqueria in Barcelona to discover a variety of local flavors. Additionally,

Costa Brava hosts numerous food festivals throughout the year, such as the Pals Rice Festival or the L'Escala Anchovy Festival, where you can savor specialty dishes and traditional treats.

Cooking Workshops And Culinary Experiences:

For those who wish to learn more about the local cuisine, Costa Brava offers cooking workshops and culinary experiences. Join a hands-on cooking class led by experienced chefs and learn to prepare traditional dishes using fresh, local ingredients. You can master the art of making paella, create your own seafood delicacies, or explore the secrets of Catalan cuisine.

Farm-To-Table Experiences:

Costa Brava's agricultural heritage is also worth exploring. Many local farms and producers offer farm-to-table experiences where visitors can learn about the cultivation of local products, such as olive oil, wine, and fruits. These experiences provide insights into sustainable farming practices and allow you to taste the flavors of the region straight from the source.

CHAPTER 6
ACCOMMODATION OPTIONS

Hotels And Resorts:

Costa Brava offers a wide range of hotels and resorts, catering to different preferences and budgets. Whether you're seeking luxury accommodations or more affordable options, there is something for everyone. Here are some notable examples:

Hotel Santa Marta (Lloret de Mar)

This luxury hotel is nestled in a serene location overlooking the Mediterranean Sea. It offers spacious rooms, a spa, multiple dining options, and access to a private beach.

Hotel Vistabella (Roses)

Situated on a beautiful cliffside, this upscale hotel provides breathtaking views of the bay and features elegant rooms, a swimming pool, a gourmet restaurant, and direct access to the beach.

Rigat Park & Spa Hotel (Lloret de Mar)

Known for its opulent ambiance, this 5-star hotel boasts luxurious suites, a spa and wellness center, an outdoor pool, and panoramic views of the surrounding landscape.

Vacation Rentals And Apartments:

For travelers seeking more space, privacy, and a home-like experience, vacation rentals and apartments are a popular choice. These options allow guests to enjoy the freedom of self-catering while immersing themselves in the local community. Here are some examples:

Airbnb

Costa Brava has a wide selection of vacation rentals listed on platforms like Airbnb, offering apartments, villas, and houses in various locations. Whether you're looking for a cozy apartment in Girona's historic center or a beachfront villa in Cadaqués, there are numerous options to choose from.

HomeAway

Similar to Airbnb, HomeAway provides a variety of vacation rentals in Costa Brava. From charming cottages in the countryside to modern apartments in coastal towns, you'll find a range of properties to suit your preferences.

Bed And Breakfasts:

Bed and breakfasts provide a more intimate and personalized accommodation experience. They often offer comfortable rooms, a homely atmosphere, and a delicious breakfast to start your day. Here are a few examples:

El Racó de Madremanya (Madremanya)

This charming bed and breakfast is set in a restored medieval farmhouse and offers cozy rooms, a garden, and a terrace. Guests can enjoy a hearty breakfast featuring local ingredients.

Can Bassa (Riudarenes)

Located in a rural setting, Can Bassa is a traditional Catalan farmhouse converted into a bed and breakfast. It features comfortable rooms, a swimming pool, a garden, and serves a delectable homemade breakfast.

Camping And Caravan Parks

Costa Brava is a haven for nature lovers, and camping and caravan parks provide an opportunity to immerse yourself in the region's beautiful landscapes. Here are a couple of examples:

Camping Internacional de Calonge (Calonge)

This family-friendly camping site offers spacious pitches for tents and caravans, as well as fully equipped bungalows. It features swimming pools, sports facilities, entertainment programs, and direct access to the beach.

Camping Riembau (Platja d'Aro)

Situated in a pine forest, this camping site offers camping pitches and mobile homes. It provides a swimming pool, sports facilities, a restaurant, and is just a short walk from the beach.

Boutique Hotels:

Costa Brava is dotted with charming boutique hotels that offer a unique and personalized experience for guests. These hotels often feature stylish decor, personalized service, and a cozy atmosphere. Some notable examples include:

Hotel Aiguaclara (Begur)

Located in the picturesque village of Begur, this boutique hotel offers individually designed rooms, a courtyard garden, and a cozy lounge area. The hotel reflects the charm of the surrounding area and provides a comfortable and intimate stay.

Hotel Hostalillo (Tamariu)

Situated in the tranquil coastal town of Tamariu, this boutique hotel offers stunning sea views, modern rooms, and direct access to the beach. Guests can enjoy a relaxing stay surrounded by the natural beauty of the Costa Brava coastline.

Rural Guesthouses:

For a peaceful and rustic retreat, Costa Brava also offers a selection of rural guesthouses. These properties are usually located in the countryside or small villages, providing an authentic and tranquil experience. Here are a couple of examples:

Mas Salvi (Pals)

Nestled in the countryside near the medieval town of Pals, Mas Salvi is a beautifully restored farmhouse offering comfortable rooms, a swimming pool, and expansive gardens. Guests can enjoy the peaceful surroundings and indulge in regional cuisine.

Can Muni (Besalú)

This charming guesthouse is located in the medieval town of Besalú and features cozy rooms, a terrace, and a restaurant. Guests can explore the historic streets of Besalú and unwind in the peaceful ambiance of Can Muni.

Eco-Lodges And Agrotourism:

For eco-conscious travelers or those interested in experiencing rural life, Costa Brava also offers eco-lodges and agrotourism accommodations. These establishments focus on sustainability, organic farming, and providing guests with an immersive rural experience. Here are a couple of examples:

Mas Pineda (Sant Pere Pescador)

This eco-lodge is set in a restored farmhouse surrounded by vineyards and olive groves. It offers comfortable rooms, a swimming pool, and an organic garden. Guests can enjoy farm-to-table meals and explore the surrounding countryside.

Can M au (Garrigoles

Located in the Empordà region, Can Mau is an agrotourism accommodation that allows guests to experience rural life on a working farm. Guests can participate in farm activities, taste local products, and enjoy the tranquility of the countryside.

CHAPTER 7
TRAVEL ITINERARIES

One Week In Costa Brava

Day 1: Girona Exploration

Start your week in Costa Brava by exploring the historic city of Girona. Walk along the ancient walls, stroll through the narrow streets of the Jewish Quarter, and visit the impressive Girona Cathedral. Don't miss a visit to the colorful houses along the Onyar River and the iconic Eiffel Bridge.

Enjoy a traditional Catalan lunch at one of the local restaurants, savoring the flavors of the region.

In the afternoon, visit the Museum of Jewish History to learn about the rich Jewish heritage of Girona. Take a leisurely walk along the city's scenic promenade, Passeig de la Muralla, which offers stunning views of the city and surrounding landscapes.

End the day by enjoying a delicious dinner at one of Girona's renowned restaurants, known for their culinary excellence.

Day 2: Coastal Beauty of Cadaqués and Cap de Creus

Travel to the charming town of Cadaqués, known for its whitewashed houses, winding streets, and beautiful coastal views. Explore the town's art galleries, visit the Church of Santa Maria, and stroll along the picturesque waterfront.

Embark on a boat trip to Cap de Creus Natural Park, a stunning coastal area with rugged cliffs, hidden coves, and crystal-clear waters. Enjoy snorkeling, swimming, or simply relaxing on the secluded beaches.

Return to Cadaqués in the evening and savor fresh seafood at one of the local restaurants, overlooking the Mediterranean Sea.

Day 3: Medieval Towns and Empordà Wine Region

Explore the medieval town of Pals, with its well-preserved historic center and panoramic views from the top of the medieval tower. Take a leisurely stroll through the cobblestone streets and visit the Romanesque Church of Sant Pere.

Head to the charming village of Peratallada, famous for its medieval architecture and stone buildings. Wander through the fortified streets, admire the castle, and enjoy a traditional Catalan lunch at a local restaurant.

In the afternoon, venture into the Empordà wine region. Visit one of the local wineries, such as Castillo Perelada or Mas Oller, for a wine tour and tasting experience. Learn about the winemaking process and sample the region's excellent wines.

Return to your accommodation and indulge in a relaxing evening, perhaps enjoying a glass of local wine while taking in the beauty of Costa Brava.

Day 4: Beaches and Water Sports in Begur and Llafranc

Spend the day exploring the stunning beaches of Begur and Llafranc. Start by visiting Sa Riera, a picturesque sandy beach with crystal-clear waters. Enjoy swimming, sunbathing, or exploring the nearby coastal paths.

Head to the scenic town of Llafranc and relax on its beautiful beach. Take a stroll along the promenade, lined with restaurants and cafes, and savor a delicious seafood lunch with a view of the Mediterranean.

If you're feeling adventurous, try your hand at water sports such as kayaking or paddleboarding, available at many of the coastal towns in Costa Brava.

End the day with a visit to the Sant Sebastià Lighthouse in Llafranc, where you can capture breathtaking views of the coastline during sunset.

Day 5: Dalí's Legacy in Figueres and Pubol

Journey to Figueres, the birthplace of renowned artist Salvador Dalí. Explore the Dalí Theatre-Museum, a surreal masterpiece showcasing Dalí's works and providing an insight into his unique artistic vision.

Continue to the medieval Castle of Gala Dalí in Pubol, once the residence of Dalí's wife, Gala. Admire the castle's architecture and explore the rooms, which contain an intriguing collection of artworks.

Take a break for a leisurely lunch at one of the local restaurants, savoring the regional cuisine.

In the afternoon, return to your accommodation and enjoy some downtime, whether it's relaxing by the pool or exploring the nearby town at your own pace.

Day 6: Natural Beauty of the Garrotxa Volcanic Zone Natural Park

Embark on a day trip to the Garrotxa Volcanic Zone Natural Park, located inland from Costa Brava. Explore the park's unique volcanic landscape, including dormant volcanoes, lava flows, and lush forests.

Visit the town of Olot, known as the gateway to the natural park. Take a walk through the charming streets, visit the Museu dels Volcans (Volcano Museum), and admire the architectural wonders of the Modernist buildings.

Enjoy a picnic amidst nature or savor a traditional Catalan meal at one of the local restaurants.

In the afternoon, hike one of the park's trails, such as the route to the Santa Margarida volcano or the Fageda d'en Jordà, a beech forest located within a volcanic crater.

Return to your accommodation and reflect on the day's adventures while enjoying a delicious dinner.

Day 7: Relaxation and Farewell

Dedicate your last day in Costa Brava to relaxation and enjoying the amenities of your accommodation. Whether it's a beachfront resort, a countryside retreat, or a boutique hotel, take the time to unwind and savor the surroundings.

Indulge in spa treatments, lounge by the pool, or take a leisurely stroll on the beach. Reflect on your week of exploration and immerse yourself in the tranquil ambiance of Costa Brava.

Enjoy a final meal at a local restaurant, relishing the flavors of the region and toasting to a memorable week in Costa Brava.

Depart with cherished memories of the stunning landscapes, vibrant culture, and warm hospitality of Costa Brava.

Two Weeks In Costa Brava

Week 1:
Days 1-3: Girona and Surroundings

Start your two-week journey in Girona, a historic city with a rich cultural heritage. Explore the enchanting Old Town, walk along the city walls, and visit the Girona Cathedral and the Arab Baths. Delight in the gastronomic scene with a visit to the local markets and restaurants.

Take a day trip to the nearby town of Besalú, known for its medieval architecture and charming streets. Explore the well-preserved Jewish Quarter, visit the 12th-century Romanesque bridge, and discover the beauty of Sant Pere Monastery.

Explore the picturesque landscapes of the Garrotxa region, including the dormant volcanoes of the Garrotxa Volcanic Zone Natural Park and the stunning beech forests of Fageda d'en Jordà.

Days 4-6: Costa Brava's Coastal Beauty

Head to the coastal town of Cadaqués, known for its whitewashed houses and artistic heritage. Visit the Salvador Dalí House-Museum in Portlligat, where the renowned artist lived and worked.

Discover the hidden coves and pristine beaches of the Cap de Creus Natural Park. Enjoy sunbathing, swimming, and snorkeling in secluded spots like Cala Jugadora and Cala Montjoi.

Continue your coastal exploration by visiting Begur and its surrounding beaches. Relax on the sandy shores of Sa Riera, Sa Tuna, and Aiguablava, and enjoy panoramic views from the medieval castle of Begur.

Don't miss a visit to the picturesque coastal towns of Tamariu, Llafranc, and Calella de Palafrugell. Stroll along the charming promenades, savor fresh seafood, and soak up the laid-back Mediterranean atmosphere.

Days 7-9: Empordà Wine Region and Cultural Delights

Embark on a wine tour in the Empordà wine region, visiting renowned wineries such as Castillo Perelada, Masia Serra, and Mas Oller. Learn about the winemaking process, sample the region's excellent wines, and indulge in delicious food pairings.

Explore the cultural gems of the region, including the Dali Theatre-Museum in Figueres, which houses an extensive collection of Salvador Dalí's artworks. Visit the Castle of Púbol, once the residence of Dalí's wife Gala, and the charming town of Pals with its medieval streets and panoramic views.

Immerse yourself in the vibrant local festivals and events that take place during your visit. Check the calendar for events like the Temps de Flors in Girona, a floral exhibition that adorns the city with vibrant displays, or the Cap Roig Festival, a renowned music festival held in the beautiful Cap Roig Gardens.

Week 2:

Days 10-12: Natural Wonders and Outdoor Adventures

Explore the breathtaking landscapes of the Montgrí Natural Park and the Medes Islands. Take a boat tour to the islands, known for their rich marine biodiversity, and enjoy activities such as snorkeling and diving.

Discover the rugged beauty of the Aiguamolls de l'Empordà Natural Park, a wetland area that is home to diverse bird species. Explore the park's trails, rent a bike, or go birdwatching.

Engage in thrilling outdoor activities such as hiking, mountain biking, or horseback riding in the stunning natural surroundings of Costa Brava. The region offers an abundance of trails and paths, including the long-distance GR 92 coastal path.

Days 13-14: Relaxation and Farewell

Dedicate the last few days of your trip to relaxation and enjoying the beaches and amenities of your chosen accommodation. Whether it's a luxurious beachfront resort, a tranquil countryside retreat, or a charming boutique hotel, unwind and soak up the serenity.

Indulge in spa treatments, lounge by the pool, or take leisurely walks on the beach. Reflect on the memorable experiences you've had throughout your two weeks in Costa Brava.

Enjoy the final evenings with exquisite dining experiences, savoring the region's gastronomic delights and raising a glass of local wine to toast to a remarkable journey.

Family-Friendly Itinerary

Day 1: Arrival and Beach Fun

Arrive in Costa Brava and settle into your family-friendly accommodation.

Spend the day relaxing and enjoying the beautiful beaches of Costa Brava. Build sandcastles, swim in the clear waters, and soak up the sun.

In the evening, explore the nearby promenades and enjoy a family dinner at a beachfront restaurant.

Day 2: Water Parks and Aquatic Adventures

Visit one of the water parks in Costa Brava, such as Water World in Lloret de Mar or Aquadiver in Platja d'Aro. Enjoy thrilling water slides, lazy rivers, and wave pools that cater to all ages.

If your family enjoys water sports, try activities like paddleboarding, kayaking, or banana boat rides, available at many coastal towns.

End the day with a delicious ice cream treat or a visit to a local gelateria.

Day 3: Exploring Medieval Towns

Visit the charming medieval town of Pals, with its narrow cobblestone streets and historic architecture. Climb to the top of the medieval tower for panoramic views.

Explore the medieval walls of Tossa de Mar and discover the impressive Vila Vella fortress. Take a walk along the town's picturesque promenade.

Enjoy a family-friendly lunch at one of the local restaurants, serving traditional Catalan dishes.

Day 4: Adventure at Adventure Parks

Spend the day at one of the adventure parks in Costa Brava, such as Parc Aventura in Sant Feliu de Guixols or Forest Park in Santa Susanna. Enjoy zip-lining, rope courses, and other thrilling activities suitable for the whole family.

Pack a picnic lunch to enjoy amidst the natural surroundings of the adventure park.

In the evening, relax at your accommodation and unwind with board games or family movie night.

Day 5: Nature and Wildlife

Explore the natural beauty of Costa Brava with a visit to the Aiguamolls de l'Empordà Natural Park. Take a guided tour or rent bikes to explore the park's diverse ecosystems and spot bird species.

Visit the Butterfly Park in Empuriabrava, where you can admire colorful butterflies and learn about their life cycle.

If your family enjoys animals, consider a visit to the Marine Animal Rescue Center in Palamós, where you can learn about the conservation efforts and see rescued marine species.

Day 6: Cultural Experiences

Discover the rich history and culture of Costa Brava with a visit to the Dalí Theatre-Museum in Figueres. Explore the surreal artworks and interactive exhibits.

Take a trip to the Toy Museum in Figueres or the Toy Museum of Catalonia in Sant Feliu de Guixols, where children can marvel at vintage toys and interactive displays.

Enjoy a family-friendly dinner at a restaurant that offers a children's menu or caters to families.

Day 7: Farewell and Last Day Adventures

Spend the last day of your family-friendly itinerary enjoying your favorite activities from the previous days or trying something new.

If time allows, take a boat trip along the coast, exploring hidden coves and enjoying the panoramic views.

Have a farewell dinner at a restaurant that offers a fun and relaxed atmosphere, allowing the whole family to enjoy a memorable final evening in Costa Brava.

Adventure And Outdoor Activities Itinerary

Day 1: Arrival and Nature Exploration

Arrive in Costa Brava and settle into your accommodation, preferably in a location close to outdoor adventure sites.

Start your adventure by exploring the stunning coastal cliffs and hiking trails of Cap de Creus Natural Park. Enjoy panoramic views of the Mediterranean Sea and immerse yourself in the rugged beauty of the landscape.

Engage in water activities like snorkeling or scuba diving in the crystal-clear waters to discover the vibrant marine life.

Day 2: Rock Climbing and Via Ferrata

Embark on a thrilling rock climbing experience in Montgrí Natural Park. Climb the limestone cliffs, accompanied by experienced guides who will ensure your safety and provide guidance.

For a more adventurous challenge, try a Via Ferrata, a protected climbing route equipped with steel cables and ladders. Conquer the cliffs while enjoying breathtaking views of the surrounding landscapes.

Day 3: Mountain Biking in the Pyrenees

Take a day trip to the Pyrenees Mountains and explore the exhilarating mountain biking trails. Enjoy the adrenaline rush as you navigate through rugged terrains, forests, and challenging descents.

Discover the beauty of nature while pedaling through picturesque landscapes, and take breaks to capture memorable photos and enjoy a picnic lunch amidst the mountain scenery.

Day 4: Sea Kayaking and Coastal Exploration

Embark on a sea kayaking adventure along the Costa Brava coastline. Paddle through hidden coves, caves, and rock formations, and explore secluded beaches accessible only by kayak.

Enjoy the tranquility of the sea, discover marine life, and take refreshing swim breaks in the crystal-clear waters. Take in the breathtaking coastal scenery and feel the exhilaration of being out on the open water.

Day 5: Paragliding and Skydiving

Experience the thrill of paragliding as you soar above the stunning landscapes of Costa Brava. Take in bird's-eye views of the coast, mountains, and countryside while enjoying a unique perspective of the region.

For the ultimate adrenaline rush, consider skydiving. Take a leap of faith from an aircraft and experience the exhilaration of freefall before parachuting safely to the ground.

Day 6: Canyoning and Whitewater Rafting

Engage in canyoning, an adventure sport that involves descending narrow canyons using a combination of hiking, climbing, and rappelling. Explore Costa Brava's canyons, navigate through waterfalls, and plunge into natural pools.

For a thrilling whitewater rafting experience, head to the Noguera Pallaresa River in the Pyrenees. Work as a team to navigate the rapids and enjoy the adrenaline rush as you conquer the white water.

Day 7: Farewell and Outdoor Relaxation

Spend your final day in Costa Brava relaxing and reflecting on your adventurous week. Choose a peaceful spot to unwind, whether it's a secluded beach, a serene forest, or a riverside location.

Take a leisurely hike or bike ride to appreciate the natural beauty of Costa Brava one last time.

Enjoy a farewell dinner at a restaurant that offers outdoor seating and delicious local cuisine, celebrating the incredible experiences and memories made during your adventure-filled week.

CHAPTER 8
PRACTICAL INFORMATION

Currency And Money Matters:

The official currency of Spain, including Costa Brava, is the Euro (€). Ensure you have some cash on hand for smaller establishments that may not accept credit cards.

ATMs are widely available throughout Costa Brava, allowing you to withdraw cash conveniently. Check with your bank about any international withdrawal fees.

Credit cards are generally accepted in most hotels, restaurants, and shops. However, it's advisable to carry some cash for smaller establishments or places that may have limited card acceptance.

Notify your bank or credit card company about your travel plans to avoid any issues with card transactions while abroad.

Language And Communication:

The official language of Costa Brava is Catalan. However, Spanish (Castilian) is widely spoken, and many locals also understand English, especially in tourist areas.

Learning a few basic phrases in Catalan or Spanish can enhance your interactions with locals and show respect for the local culture.

Consider using translation apps or carrying a pocket-sized phrasebook to assist with communication in case of language barriers.

Health And Safety:

Costa Brava generally has good healthcare facilities and services. However, it's recommended to have travel insurance that covers medical expenses and emergency evacuation.

Carry any necessary prescription medications in their original containers and bring a copy of your prescriptions.

Ensure you have appropriate travel vaccinations before your trip and check the latest travel advisories and health recommendations for the region.

Take necessary precautions to protect yourself from the sun, such as using sunscreen, wearing a hat, and staying hydrated.

Customs And Etiquette:

Spanish and Catalan cultures have their own customs and etiquette. It's polite to greet people with a handshake or kiss on both cheeks, especially when meeting for the first time.

Dining etiquette typically involves keeping your hands on the table and waiting for the host to begin eating before you start.

Tipping is customary in restaurants, with 10% of the bill considered a standard tip. However, review the bill to check if a service charge is already included.

Dress appropriately when visiting religious sites or participating in cultural events. Modest clothing is generally expected, with shoulders and knees covered.

CHAPTER 9
TRAVEL TIPS AND RECOMMENDATIONS

Must-See Attractions In Costa Brava:

Dali Theatre-Museum (Figueres)
Explore the surreal world of Salvador Dalí at this captivating museum, which showcases a vast collection of his artwork and provides insight into his creative genius.

Tossa de Mar
This picturesque coastal town is known for its medieval fortress, Vila Vella, offering panoramic views of the sea. Stroll through the charming old town, relax on its beautiful beaches, and savor fresh seafood in waterfront restaurants.

Girona
Discover the historic charm of Girona, with its well-preserved medieval walls, narrow streets,

and impressive Cathedral. Explore the Jewish Quarter, visit the Arab Baths, and enjoy the vibrant atmosphere of the city's squares and cafes.

Cap de Creus Natural Park

Experience the rugged beauty of this protected area, where dramatic cliffs meet the turquoise waters of the Mediterranean. Hike along scenic trails, visit the picturesque lighthouse, and take in breathtaking panoramic views.

Cadaqués:

A picturesque coastal village that has attracted artists and writers for decades. Wander through its narrow streets, admire the white-washed houses, and visit the house of Salvador Dalí, which is now a museum.

Hidden Gems In Costa Brava:

Begur

A charming town with beautiful beaches and a medieval castle. Enjoy its narrow streets, hidden coves, and panoramic viewpoints that offer stunning vistas of the coastline.

Cala S'Alguer (Palamos)

A hidden gem, this small fishing village is a peaceful oasis with colorful fishermen's houses and a charming beach. Enjoy a tranquil day by the sea and savor the local cuisine at its seafood restaurants.

Sant Martí d'Empúries

This small coastal village is home to the impressive ruins of the ancient Greek and Roman city of Empúries. Explore the archaeological site and stroll along the sandy beaches nearby.

Tamariu

A picturesque fishing village with a beautiful crescent-shaped beach and crystal-clear waters. Enjoy its relaxed atmosphere, sample delicious seafood, and take a boat trip along the coastline.

Monastery of Sant Pere de Rodes

Located in the mountains near Port de la Selva, this medieval monastery offers stunning views of the surrounding landscape. Explore its impressive architecture, visit the church, and enjoy the peaceful ambiance.

Local Experiences And Activities

Wine Tasting in Empordà
Costa Brava is home to the Empordà wine region, known for its exceptional wines. Embark on a wine tasting tour, visit local vineyards, and sample the region's renowned reds, whites, and sparkling wines. Learn about the winemaking process and indulge in delicious food pairings.

Local Food Tours
Explore the culinary delights of Costa Brava through food tours that take you to local markets, bakeries, and traditional restaurants. Sample regional specialties such as paella, fideuà (a seafood dish), and suquet de peix (fish stew), and learn about the local ingredients and cooking techniques.

Traditional Festivals
Immerse yourself in the vibrant local culture by attending traditional festivals and events. Costa Brava hosts various festivals throughout the year, such as the Carnival in February, the Sant Joan celebration in June, and the Festa Major in

different towns. Experience lively parades, music, dancing, and traditional costumes.

Outdoor Concerts and Performances

During the summer months, many towns in Costa Brava host outdoor concerts and performances. Enjoy live music, theater, and dance shows in stunning settings, such as historic squares, castle courtyards, or beachside stages. Check the local event calendars for upcoming performances.

Water Sports and Sailing

Take advantage of Costa Brava's beautiful coastline and engage in water sports such as snorkeling, scuba diving, windsurfing, or paddleboarding. Alternatively, charter a boat or join a sailing excursion to explore hidden coves, remote beaches, and scenic coastal landscapes.

CHAPTER 10 SHOPPING AND SOUVENIRS

Local Markets

Explore the vibrant local markets in Costa Brava, such as the Mercat de la Boqueria in Barcelona or the Mercat de Palafrugell. Discover a wide array of fresh produce, local delicacies, crafts, and souvenirs. Pick up traditional items like ceramics, textiles, or handmade jewelry.

Handcrafted Goods

Costa Brava is known for its traditional craftsmanship. Look for unique handcrafted items such as ceramics from La Bisbal, espadrilles (traditional canvas shoes) from Peratallada, or handwoven baskets from Palamos. These make wonderful souvenirs or gifts.

Gastronomic Souvenirs

Bring home the flavors of Costa Brava by purchasing local food products like olive oil, saffron, cured meats, or artisanal cheeses. Visit specialty food shops or markets to find high-quality products that reflect the region's culinary traditions.

Art And Photography

Explore local art galleries and studios to find unique pieces of artwork or photography inspired by Costa Brava's natural beauty and cultural heritage. Support local artists and bring home a one-of-a-kind souvenir that captures the essence of the region.

CHAPTER 11 PHOTOGRAPHY AND INSTAGRAM SPOTS

Els Àngels Sanctuary (Girona)

Capture breathtaking panoramic views of Girona and the surrounding landscapes from this hilltop sanctuary. The viewpoint offers stunning photo opportunities, especially during sunrise or sunset.

Cala Banys (Lloret De Mar)

This small rocky cove offers a picturesque setting for photography. Capture the dramatic cliffs, turquoise waters, and the charming bar perched on the rocks. It's especially stunning during golden hour.

Besalú

Explore the medieval town of Besalú, known for its well-preserved architecture and iconic bridge. Wander through its narrow streets, capture the historic buildings, and photograph the bridge reflected in the river.

Sant Sebastià Lighthouse (Llafranc)

Located on a cliff overlooking the Mediterranean, this lighthouse provides a stunning backdrop for photography. Capture the rugged coastline, the lighthouse tower, and the mesmerizing sea views.

Cap Roig Botanical Garden (Calella De Palafrugell)

Discover a variety of exotic plants, sculptures, and terraced gardens in this scenic botanical garden. Explore the different areas, including the amphitheater with panoramic views, and capture its natural beauty.

Remember to respect local guidelines and regulations when visiting these spots, and always be mindful of the environment and the privacy of others.

Printed in Great Britain
by Amazon